Marc Vincenz

Einstein Fledermaus

SurVision Books

First published in 2021 by
SurVision Books
Dublin, Ireland
Reggio di Calabria, Italy
www.survisionmagazine.com

Copyright © Marc Vincenz, 2021

Cover image: *Mayan Paranuit* by Sophia Santos
Copyright © Sophia Santos, 2021

Design © SurVision Books, 2021

ISBN: 978-1-912963-20-1

This book is in copyright. No part of this publication may be reproduced, stored in a retrieval system, or transmitted in any form or by any means without the prior permission in writing from the publisher.

Acknowledgments

Grateful acknowledgement is made to the editors of the following, in which some of these poems, or versions of them, originally appeared:

Beltway Poetry Quarterly (USA): "The Patent Lawyer Had It Wrong," "Listen to the Drums," "All the Stops," and "Shifting Planktons of Later Joy."

Westerly Magazine (Australia): *"Switzerland 911"*

Axon: Creative Explorations (Australia): "Unlearning the Ropes," "Evidence of Impropriety," and "Household Speak"

SurVision (Ireland): "King Rat in Little City" and "Sleepless Night"

spoKe 9 (USA): "Le Flâneur in Uneven Years," "Undying Love Tentacles," "An Undoing, Or at Three am in the Pharmacy in a Big City on the Ocean," and "Upwardly Mobile"

Contents

Act One. EINSTEIN'S APARTMENT

The Patent Lawyer Had It Wrong	7
Listen to the Drums	8
All the Stops	9
Shifting Planktons of Later Joy	10
A Short Meditation on Birdsong	12
Switzerland 911	13
Obviate	14

Act Two. A SUMMER HOUSE IN THE VILLA ORLOFSKY

A Summer House in the Villa Orlofsky	15
Toward the Holy Land	16
There Were 14 Angels	17
Unlearning the Ropes	18
Heavy Water	19
Liquefaction	20
At the Bank	21
Visa Application	22
Amorous Songs to the Universe	23
The Undertaker	24
Evidence of Impropriety	25
Household Speak	26
Upwardly Mobile	27

Act Three. IN THE PRISON OFFICES OF WARDEN FRANK

Everything I Ever Dreamed Of	28
To a Fellow Traveler	29
Sleepless Night	30
Upstanding Citizen	31

An Undoing; Or, At Three a.m. in the Pharmacy
   in a Big City on the Ocean   32
King Rat in Little City   33
Oil of Sanctification   34
An Offshoot   35
Back in the City   36
Le Flâneur in Uneven Years   37

Dénouement

Undying Love Tentacles   38

*I always get by with my naiveté,
which is at best 20 percent deliberate.*

—Albert Einstein

*You are quite inhuman!
You rant as in a feverfrenzy
And gobble like a turkeycock!*

—Johann Strauss II, Act 1, *Die Fledermaus*

Act One. EINSTEIN'S APARTMENT

The Patent Lawyer Had It Wrong

Francesca, Georg's sister, had the following to say
in her somewhat sinister way. They were all forgeries,
she said, then turned to the balcony that looked
out on an empty dock—the swishing of the waves
was a dead giveaway; it was her inclement way
of saying, This doesn't have what it takes.
And I said, Vendetta will get the better of you, my
Sweet Rabbit. Even when you purse your lips
into a colon, there's little at the end of it.
no hyphen, simply a word: convention.

If that was really the end of it, I should have
been surprised. I shouldn't mention the honors
now conferred upon me; the laurel leaves abound my
ears as if we still had a Senate majority
or a judiciary; as if we still had those shrunken
heads Pa brought back from the Philippines,
and those old souls might convey—withholding
all their pink slips—a modicum of fantasy-cum-
factdom. Who cares? It's all made up anyway.

Listen to the Drums

The glances that survive are these: a fluid
motion, really, clearly one that says this geographic frenzy
stops the slightest flickering of lashes.

I know you to be the belle of the ball.

You know, of course, the body of the state
is tied up in you. Nothing can be given away.
Show me your barcode and the secrets it keeps.

All the Stops

Those erroneous myths of the sheep and the man, the man and the cow, the cow and the cowl; forget the man, move to the sea, over mountain, dale and creek, move to the graduations, to the geographic tongue or the archipelago of mind-time, space, the mythological frontier of civilization and the stars; or the cow leaping over the moon, or the stork on her way to the newborn, or the man in the moon who is also rabbit or hare, who passes messages to those of us who care to hear. And yet, here I stand, not enormous, but small, living in the longing.

Shifting Planktons of Later Joy

Who hasn't drunk from the upland fountains
where fresh hazel is cut each night, or deep
in the brook, long past migration time, a cloud
of steel wool crosses the landscape; the butterflies

have gone, the wolf dwells in his lair, the bear,
unafraid of anything except chocolate, licks
her paws. Are there any shepherds left here?
Back in town, Latin is spoken in the tavernas

and the underground chambers where light
plumbing coughs and sneezes, where the scaffolding
holds the mirror image, left-right-hand-left,
of the State. Here's Mildred in her pajamas

twisting her legs into a state of rest, there's
Jonathan in his slippers shuffling through the day;
and here's Jennifer all made out in pink and red,
a rose petal presenting her fair share of newspaper

clippings—engorged in the cover of *People*
or *Life*, in the paraphyletic of the *Daily News*—
all speed variance accounted for, held in deep
esteem and sway, converged this way,

up the down scale, unfettered, fitting and free,
making history on her own scale, up means down;
gravity is like pleurisy, a shriek from the future
we expected and interjected, inserted

and squirted into the melee, our spirits slashing
for the first audience with the anointed one;
oh the drama, the preposterous proposition
when a grapnel clutches your car dripping

from the river, and the wind-up creature
in your sights swerves to the right; discursive
this whole affair. Poetry, of course,
is an attack on violent forces.

A Short Meditation on Birdsong

All the models of creation were concerned
with meaning and purpose, at least in this
human's mind. All those floating hands,
the blessing conferred; but for a moment, just
listen, find your longing. All the models
of creation are metaphors; all those waves
sweeping space trying to find a melody,
all those words simply a place to put your harvest,
all those feathers, wings charging up;
all the longing fingers; over the mountain,
via the mailman, the words; the language
of the birds, in truth a model emanation
with meaning and purpose—and so the day
flew by in all her graces, sun-high, rain in the nodes.

Switzerland 911

All hail the Alps and their glassine ice-stream, the *Stube* with her calvados and *Kaffeecreme*, or the sausages air-dried in glacial attics in every barn across the heartland; oh, and the cheeses, the little holes that harbor untold secrets even from the magic of physics. Outside, watch the Ibex ascend the tallest crags like stairs. One night we are drinking beers and *Kirsch*, playing blackjack with American tourists. *What did they call it? Six-card stud?* And Armin, decked out in his Swiss Army uniform. The epaulette put him at the rank of Colonel, a leader of men and machines in the hearty mountain division. All hail the Alps and their hollowed out interiors—some place in the Vaud there's an entire city embedded in the mountain below the chasm, cleared for centuries by avalanches and foxes, and lone bobcats who pounce for field mice. On the central square inside the mountain city, there is a soccer field where the goal posts are just a few feet further apart, and Alesh, the local policeman dribbles his way toward the end line. *Tor! Tor!* are the cheers that echo Thursday nights across the valley. Finally, you light a cigar and the smoke finds its way up the stairs. On your way up you give me a wink and a note. *My room is 911*, it says. I bow out of the last hand, fold on a perfect bobtail straight. For you the idea of time is self-evident. It must be spent before ascending those final steps where birds migrate the Milky Way, or deep into the liquid of mathematics all compasses pointing true north. So up I arise, engineering and economics leading the way, and in 911, your navel becomes the heart of the galaxy, a black hole collapsing in on itself, all those calvados atoms swirling in a haze of Swiss bravado.

Obviate

All the cobwebs swept away, everything comes into clear focus. The mouse, watch the mouse; know these poems represent nothing more than the bourgeois concerns of the makeup artist and the stationmaster, the noise of the policeman and the stand-up comedian. All told, the universe repels attraction; something like the hunter's vest with all its zips and Velcro, the slips and trips of etiquette, the clang of the anvil, the stationmaster's whistle.

Act Two. A SUMMER HOUSE IN THE VILLA ORLOFSKY

A Summer House in the Villa Orlofsky

Black fabric against the wind. Those deeds are unbecoming, the torn handkerchief in the jacket pocket, the old hair and dandruff on the shoulders, the smell of pipe tobacco, a vanilla that permeates everything. "What I am dreaming of is a house in the valley," you say applying your lipstick. Black gears were clicking into position. Swallowing any modicum of discretion, I say, "Yes, let's fuck." There was dynamite in my veins, or perhaps it was that hot bath I took at lunchtime; "Now let's move on," I say. Black fabric against the mind. "Do we need a translator?" you say. I say, "Yes. We need those neurons to keep their impartial wisdom." You poured a glass of sangria from a ceramic jug, then winked.

Toward the Holy Land

Jerusalem was a place placed in my mind like a jewel in the lotus flower, a holy grail, a shooting star, a meteor, the flow of the Milky Way where with a single word we are held hostage. And who would forget the right hand thrumming the bar stool, the hollow sound of dead bone, or the pages, the thousands upon thousands of pages disappeared. The English say they came to this place to write history, not for the jackals or the foxes, not for the mangy lions and their filigree of weeds; of course, the first word was good. *Get them out there and preach the word. Doesn't everything lead us there, to the Holy Land?* The home I seek is other. She spreads her boundaries on a shard of pottery or a glazed beaker that has been blessed by Greek and Roman and Egyptian wine, by the words of philosophers, the seers and the sayers; all those folks climbing ivy breathing hot, afraid of sudden death but clinging to the crevices, the outcrops like the goats in their hard toes; the running across clifftops, over the thinnest jigsaw of geology; out of the ground, the difference between distance and come-here-alone. *Sit down, take a breather. Today is the day you will finally blow your own horn, but try to remember, Thou shalt not want, thou shalt lie low inside the house, dwell in the old landscape among the mice and the lice.*

There Were 14 Angels

God pays his worshipers in coconut oil tonight. The burnt grass on the incline grew there. Indignation too is a language. "I'll give you a thousand pounds, "he said, "to change the language." "Don't stop with them," you said, "one of these other nights you will hear the piano playing a melody nearby—as if seashells could speak to an empty home." "The world collapses, and yet you talk of those deep caves in her wide eyes," you said. Nothing could have been further from the truth. "How would *you* like it," you said, "if the olive in the martini ended up in your beard. There are those who pass by in the middle of the night who never pay a dime." And there was me, I, *ich, moi, je ne sai croire,* attempting a semblance of normalcy. Then, out of the suburbs of nothingness with their blank cars and groomed dogs, the cats, the ever-shitting cats. Remember there were once one thousand angels and now there are only 14. Is that a reason to rejoice? Remember, you have to finish that cocktail before you go to sleep. For every living apple there is an unfair trade in language and imagination. Let's meet at the river's edge, let us succor to the limit of it. Unwind the word of it. Was there ever a better time to write my repertoire. Never a word of it, the undoing of it ends you up in the drink.

Unlearning the Ropes

"The Republic," they say, "must be upheld at all costs." Thousands of fates are at stake, but almost no advice. "What are your demands?" they say. "Know we are prepared to serve any loss as long as you stay six feet away." Her apathy is reflected in her face as she doles out soup and buttered bread. "Which cloud?" she says scattering a handful of parmesan. The old man sighs, remembering last summer when the bamboo reeds were green, remembering the abundance of bees. "All of their prophecies come true," he says blowing on his spoon.

Heavy Water

Everything measured can be seen from the outside. We work slowly in blown glass and cut crystal. Someplace else, the rain is no more; the old handle on the winch creaks and whines, the bucket is dry. What great freedom have we won ourselves with this, he thinks. Out in the pasture, the weeds are taking over, the cows have xylophones for ribs, the earth, parched, is singing: "Reach for the black oil inside me."

Liquefaction

Like Van Gogh, we reach for the perfect line or spiral. You will have heard that we once amused ourselves in our white winter fleece with clouds floating outward. We wished to swim in the clouds, wanted to give the wasteland new color, but scaffolding rose to block the view. But soon, the clock strikes six and a cloud of dust from the galaxy, or a lightness, or some strange form of happiness makes me go out into the woods. I count the naked minutes out here listening to bark scrape over a whole epoch of lines. "You know nothing of love," the lines seem to say. A raccoon comes into the picture with all her whiskers; she stirs beneath the trees like she's making a soup. Far beneath, the mouse sleeps in her hollows, meanwhile the snow falls coating every surface with her tiny under-feathers. Suddenly everything comes into focus. In an instant, a spray of faces: Audrey Hepburn, Marilyn, Jimmy Dean, Clark Gable, even Rudolph Valentino on the silent screen in his pantaloons, knee-high boots and a saber. Tarzan yodels, swinging wildly with his monkeys in ways you have never seen. Your footprints in the snow. All clear evidence you have been here once before.

At the Bank

Filing patents is an expensive business. How do you define a wavelength of light to the common eye? Or the speed of such in its in and out, its out and in, its inside out from within? Dear Sir, please acknowledge all documents received heretofore. You know there's more to come. "Fill your pockets with light," he says offering me a glass of pink bitters with a slice of lemon on the side. "You forgot the combination," he says in a sly smile. "Were we not about to look into the secret space of creation? How can you put a number on that?" "Nothing filled out, nothing gained, "you say and hope to leave it at that. I hesitate to put this on paper, but filing patents is an expensive business, so you raise your glass and say: "Good riddance to all that."

Visa Application

More paperwork with boxes. Does the X mean what it says, and the tick is more than a tick, but a flea in the ear rather than a fly in the ointment, an upturned star, both legs reaching up and all-embracing, a resolute 'yes'. Does the paperwork come in boxes? Who knows what she says—yes, she with the horn-rimmed glasses, she with the cockamamie smile. The flea in your ear was rattling and buzzing and uncorking your mind. What was it she said? "I have all the boxes. What do you have?"

Amorous Songs to the Universe

Absence and presence as written in the Tao Te Ching is like foresight and hindsight. What lies in between but Dark Matter. Another way of looking at this is: Who resides in the mirror but you. All the bureaucrats are sipping Ouzo in the Café Royale after midnight. It seems the Greeks knew a thing or two. Lemon and garlic are the perfect pairing of bring out the flavor of any meat or bean, the perfect pairing to cleave the dusk to dawn. By this time the tables were full of foot-stomping song, and at that critical moment, after a Davidoff more or two, something became clear—an epiphany? A liturgy? The question wasn't whose home to awaken in. Given all this time meditating on the question you had to know where the answer was coming from. God singing into the cosmos. It was at the Kaiser Bar on Hauptallee behind the Rathhaus where crows gathered in the dawn to fight over the remnants of a mouse, where during the day, the children dragged their tubas, their bassoons, their xylophone mallets and their flugelhorns to practice "The Good Lord Is within Us." And what I am given to understand is, He was. The cosmos itself (or themselves) is continuously tumbling through its transformations. I should know this better than most.

The Undertaker

Autumn eats out of her orchards.

A carp's eye appears at the surface of the lake.

The fountains are still.

Baked bread in the air.

There was a moment when I wanted to pull my hair out, but then I realized it's all gone like the death of Osiris and all these dreams of wilded plains rich in insects and hares.

If someone has something to say, simply say it.

There are few words at all, if any, at a time like this.

As it turns out, you're always opening the door, and letting what is in, out.

The fair hair of the woman in the pinstripe suit caught the light, and then it stayed there.

Evidence of Impropriety

Via the Via Canale, near the Orpietto, at the shore, an elephant passes by; on her head, ripe oranges in a golden bowl. A grandmother crosses the road as herself. "Receive or transmit me," she says. "How can an elephant live in Italy without being lonely?" she says.

Household Speak

The language she spoke was soft and uniform but unlike anything I had heard before. She called to mind my Great Aunt Lorelei; she who wore those soft summer roses everywhere. I wished I could decipher each nuance and phrase, each of her tongue movements and the air in her mouth. Truth be told, as I later learned, what she said, although seemingly from another galaxy, some strange star constellation where every planet had two stars of its own, and to whom one hundred years was a thousand of our own. The twinned suns of the Holileese; and no, they had no laser guns or free speech. They lived in hollow chambers beneath the surface of their planet and they counted stars and sheep, just like us. Still, she spoke, uninterrupted, and her voice cast a shadow or a shade—whichever way one might look at it—"Water is always level," I heard she had said, or I heard speak of such things. On the other hand, someone said, over another glass of cognac and a cigarette, "These things are often overblown. I hear she was a grass grower." "That would explain the tone," I said.

Upwardly Mobile

The summer burdens. See how the fisherman turns the rudder efficiently. News comes from nowhere. We don't know whether to rest or sleep. "You weren't married when we made this vow," he says. "The burden is too much to bear. Time refracts, and behind us a monastery opens!" "Who knew you were still here!" someone calls. All ears burn open, and this is what was said: "Return to the mountains and the rivers, to the trout and their spawn, to the soaring of the buzzards. The early bird sings for himself alone."

Act Three. IN THE PRISON OFFICES OF WARDEN FRANK

Everything I Ever Dreamed Of

And thus the serpent seduces the seducer, entices the fruit to take shape inside the mind, the original sear of fire on skin, the ebb and flow of breath at that secret place of creation. A cluster of young balls of gas burning helium and hydrogen are the mark of the celestial bull standing his pasture, staring down the Man in the Moon and the Earth in all of God's creation. Was this the same who misguided us in the labyrinth or whom the Minoans bounded over in their bloodthirsty rites? Or the savage who faced us against the walls of Pamplona? Can you imagine all that vegan power muscled up. A protector who has no fear of knives or skewers or the fluffing up of red curtains that hide the maker. Who says you need to swirl around a star to understand all this?

To a Fellow Traveler

Don't follow the beaten path; strike out into unknown pastures. Watch the buds open meticulously; all the secrets are hidden in the light and how it enters the eyes. You can't smell the cosmos, say you? Or perhaps you can in the dampness of the leaves and hear it in the snap of the twigs beneath your feet, in the playful dance of the butterflies, or feel it in the steam rising from the deep. Nothing that crosses your face lies, here the power resides in the heart of a planet, in its fathoming-self climbing to gaze out. Who doesn't love a grand view? Either way, one day you shall encounter the language that speaks in numbers to describe the cosmos, and they will fly, not migrate, no, but soar above the mountains and the clouds, and further still into dark space. Watch the mind carry itself universes away—perhaps it's possible to split light and create two shadows, one that's here and one that's far away, and then to look into that world and hope that all our geometric facets exist everywhere, just like energy, just like mystery. Dear fellow traveler, I wish you well on your discoveries—a merchant ship sailing into your own dark enigma. The mind needs something to fix upon.

Sleepless Night

Dark storms brooding, bats fly out in the night; they circle the moon briefly before veering off. You sit here on my chest looming. Are you Fuseli's ghost? Or perhaps you are part of a dream that never surfaces? Or Sisyphus rolling his boulder uphill again and again? Or the dark tirades of Mongolian warlords? Certainly you are part of the vast sphere of the universe. Cooling down, words become atoms, become whole worlds circling suns, become ether or dark matter, become the transmutation of thought. Someone once said, "It is in the experience that the thing lives itself." Observe the chrysanthemum, they weave our true selves into the sky. Ah, these chasers of ellipses, I say. The probability exists even more than mountains.

Upstanding Citizen

Up at the crack of dawn; the heartache has gone now. You remain proud and unvanquished like the owl on his perch or the thorned branches he clutches in his talons. An unredeemed sacrifice is his deathless victory; but seriously, can he tell you how the world works? Collect them all together, under one roof, under the dome of blue earth. Ask the augurs, the shaman, the fakirs, the railroad workers, ask the bartenders on the Upper East Side, the Hong Kong tailors, the chambermaids, the surveyors, the sailors, ask the manicurists and the ornithologists, or those who write letters on roads; ask them one and all: What makes you one of the good ones?

An Undoing; or, At Three a.m. in the Pharmacy in a Big City on the Ocean

Reflexology. Ornithology. Radiology.
Three things that strike a pose in me.

See how my toes curl! Don't forget,
you'll have an agenda too, I guess.

The wide-eye claims of the extinction
of the dodo is something they just

can't abide. Why the dodo thrives
at every corner store and gasoline station.

Three dollars for a gallon and two more
cents for a glazed donut. Eat it in

the moonshine, under the pines,
on the park benches. See how

the ferns bow, watch the puffed-up
plastic bags rise to the light like jellyfish, and listen

to the incessant clamoring and chittering
of all those damn squirrels and crickets.

King Rat in Little City

Shuffling the chips, he says: "The lamp of reason does not illuminate these children. Of all those who have come before—Chairman of the Royal Society, indeed." At a lecture on the role of the primate in agrarian society, he says: "This one time, an unfamiliar glow erupted. It's all about the critical mass, the raisins in the porridge. But I assure you, this is no Russian roulette. Whatever emerges spontaneously shall be considered the true undertaking."

I wrote you a letter, Doctor King Rat, perfectly formed in the shape of a rotten cabbage. You say the lamp of reason does not illuminate, and I hear you say that in God's name. A sword is a sword is a sword, I say.

Oil of Sanctification

The breath of a sleeping infant,
the noise of children playing,
the garden watching over her fruit,
the mountain forests deep in shadow greens,
the deconstruction of logical three-dimensional space,
the subjective terrain of the human mind,
the emptiness at the river's surface,
numbers interwoven in the uncountable,
a lone moon buffeted on tumbling waves,
the exoskeleton of some kind of scorpion,
the root system deep beneath our feet,
the pressure points along the spine,
the final self-portrait in the dark,
the oily egg-whipped colors, only whole
on the outside, the wind stirring, the holy-
sanctified, a stretch of mozzarella cheese,
a less-willful breeze, an upright walking man,
a man on his knees, a woman with wings
flying in the air, no strings, no measure
this autumn equinox. Ducks and geese
set off everywhere.

An Offshoot

Three moonless nights
and the coyotes are out at dawn.
Somewhere in the ocean
the eels are lost,
turning into seaweed.

Back in the City

No longer exposed to the moon's changing cycles;
everything is illuminated in camphor and phosphor,
in sulfur and carbon dioxide, radioactive waves
of invisible power raining down. Absence is a kind
of emergence. Sea cucumbers line the curbs,
searching for trace elements of brine, ducks peck
their way down the roads, and, especially
on a Friday night when garters are exposed,
the old pissoir reeks of childhood memory, rank
but comforting, like a blue cheese growing old.

Le Flâneur in Uneven Years

Stones fell out of the air, it was the 19th century and the salons were a flurry in chamber quartets, powdered sleeves and curls, the atom had yet to be discovered and everything was all ether and the search for the soul. Immortality seemed less likely even though you had dragon eggs, an ample supply of magical tincture, and the eyelash of a cyclops. The wildlife was skittish, a halo of snow burned into a perfect crucible. The people from far afield and further away in their fancy wigs and glasses spilling over with wine shot out into the warm breeze with their horse-drawn carriages. Stones fell out of the air in the 21st century and the bars were crammed full of beer and baseball, ouzo and osso buco, little canapés with pickled shrimp and crab. Brand-building time: a blissful shade among the daisies sipping orange soda, everything at arm's length—along list for a lost cause. There's Uncle Fortunato locked up on a misdemeanor, Auntie Josephina with her wild nights and wiry hair, and Cousin Jacob styling himself as a Comanche Chief on Times Square, or Cousin Suzella in her eye makeup and stilettos scooping dogshit at creek. What do I know of this? When the mountain spoke to the lake, she spoke in stones.

Dénouement

Undying Love Tentacles

Just a glimpse, a fragment that holds resonance.

A choir of angels glorify the moment.

A viper slithers through tall grass.

Ten thousand miles of radiant fields.

A sticky music flows slowly deep into tissue—
all those jelly-filled canals, radical pairs sensing the
vibrations in the earth's magnetic field.

Out in the ocean, birds, whales and turtles migrate,
give birth, until they drift into sleep.

Falling stars flare on the river.

More poetry published by SurVision Books

Noelle Kocot. *Humanity*
(New Poetics: USA)
ISBN 978-1-9995903-0-7

Ciaran O'Driscoll. *The Speaking Trees*
(New Poetics: Ireland)
ISBN 978-1-9995903-1-4

Helen Ivory. *Maps of the Abandoned City*
(New Poetics: England)
ISBN 978-1-912963-04-1

Elin O'Hara Slavick. *Cameramouth*
(New Poetics: USA)
ISBN 978-1-9995903-4-5

John W. Sexton. *Inverted Night*
(New Poetics: Ireland)
ISBN 978-1-912963-05-8

Afric McGlinchey. *Invisible Insane*
(New Poetics: Ireland)
ISBN 978-1-9995903-3-8

Anatoly Kudryavitsky. *Stowaway*
(New Poetics: Ireland)
ISBN 978-1-9995903-2-1

Tim Murphy. *The Cacti Do Not Move*
(New Poetics: Ireland)
ISBN 978-1-912963-07-2

Tony Kitt. *The Magic Phlute*
(New Poetics: Ireland)
ISBN 978-1-912963-08-9

Clayre Benzadón. *Liminal Zenith*
(New Poetics: USA)
ISBN 978-1-912963-11-9

Thomas Townsley. *Tangent of Ardency*
(New Poetics: USA)
ISBN 978-1-912963-15-7

Matthew Geden. *Fruit*
(New Poetics: Ireland)
ISBN 978-1-912963-16-4

George Kalamaras. *That Moment of Wept*
ISBN 978-1-9995903-7-6

Anton Yakovlev. *Chronos Dines Alone*
(Winner of James Tate Poetry Prize 2018)
ISBN 978-1-912963-01-0

Bob Lucky. *Conversation Starters in a Language No One Speaks*
(Winner of James Tate Poetry Prize 2018)
ISBN 978-1-912963-00-3

Christopher Prewitt. *Paradise Hammer*
(Winner of James Tate Poetry Prize 2018)
ISBN 978-1-9995903-9-0

Mikko Harvey & Jake Bauer. *Idaho Falls*
(Winner of James Tate Poetry Prize 2018)
ISBN 978-1-912963-02-7

Tony Bailie. *Mountain Under Heaven*
(Winner of James Tate Poetry Prize 2019)
ISBN 978-1-912963-09-6

Nicholas Alexander Hayes. *Amorphous Organics*
(Winner of James Tate Poetry Prize 2019)
ISBN 978-1-912963-10-2

John Bradley. *Spontaneous Mummification*
(Winner of James Tate Poetry Prize 2019)
ISBN 978-1-912963-13-3

John Thomas Allen. *Rolling in the Third Eye*
(Winner of James Tate Poetry Prize 2019)
ISBN 978-1-912963-15-7

Gary Glauber. *The Covalence of Equanimity*
(Winner of James Tate Poetry Prize 2019)
ISBN 978-1-912963-12-6

Maria Grazia Calandrone. *Fossils*
Translated from Italian
(New Poetics: Italy)
ISBN 978-1-9995903-6-9

Sergey Biryukov. *Transformations*
Translated from Russian
(New Poetics: Russia)
ISBN 978-1-9995903-5-2

Alexander Korotko. *Irrazionalismo*
Translated from Russian
(New Poetics: Ukraine)
ISBN 978-1-912963-06-5

Anton G. Leitner. *Selected Poems 1981–2015*
Translated from German
ISBN 978-1-9995903-8-3

message-door: An Anthology of Contemporary Surrealist Poetry from Russia (bilingual)
Edited and translated from Russian by Anatoly Kudryavitsky
ISBN 978-1-912963-17-1

Seeds of Gravity: An Anthology of Contemporary Surrealist Poetry from Ireland
Edited by Anatoly Kudryavitsky
ISBN 978-1-912963-18-8

All our books are available to order via
http://survisionmagazine.com/books.htm